Barbers

by Alison Behnke

⌐ Lerner Publications Company • Minneapolis

Special thanks to the Moler Barber School of Hairstyling

Lerner Publications Company
A division of Lerner Publishing Group
241 First Avenue North
Minneapolis, MN 55401 U.S.A.

Website address: www.lernerbooks.com

Words in **bold type** are explained in a glossary on page 31.

Library of Congress Cataloging-in-Publication Data

Behnke, Alison.
    Barbers / by Alison Behnke.
        p.   cm. – (Pull ahead books)
    Includes index.
    ISBN-13: 978–0–8225–2799–2 (lib. bdg. : alk. paper)
    ISBN-10: 0–8225–2799–5 (lib. bdg. : alk. paper)
        1. Barbering–Juvenile literature. 2. Barbershops–
Juvenile literature. I. Title. II. Series.
    TT957.B38 2006
    646.7'24'092–dc22   2005004329

Manufactured in the United States of America
1 2 3 4 5 6 – JR – 11 10 09 08 07 06

Your hair is getting pretty long. Maybe you need it cut. Who should you visit?

The barber!

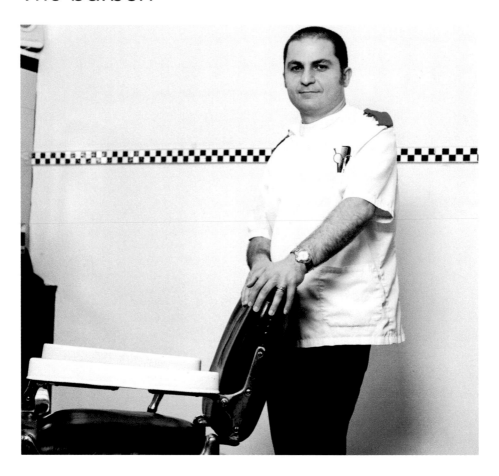

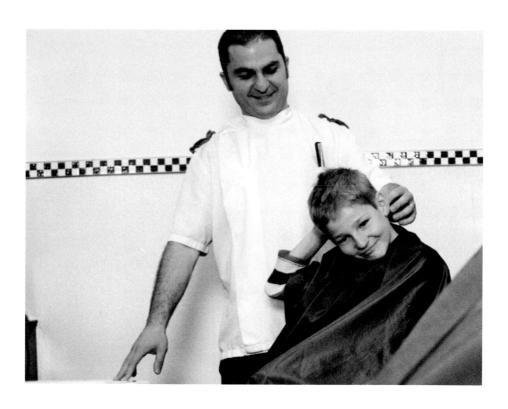

The barber works in a shop in your **community**. Your community is made up of people in your neighborhood, town, or city.

Some barbershops are old and some are new. Some barbers work in big shops.

Other
barbershops
are small.
They might
have only
two or three
chairs.

Barbers have had lots of **training**. Training teaches them how to do their job.

Most barbers train at special schools. These schools teach people how to cut hair.

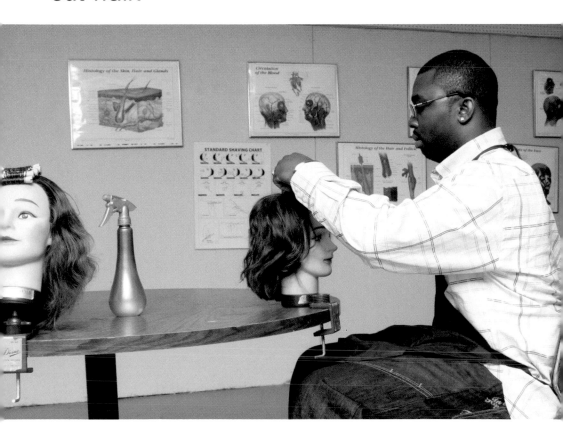

Many different **customers** come to see the barber.

Customers are people who visit the barber to get haircuts or to have other work done.

The barber asks customers what they would like done.

Some just want haircuts.

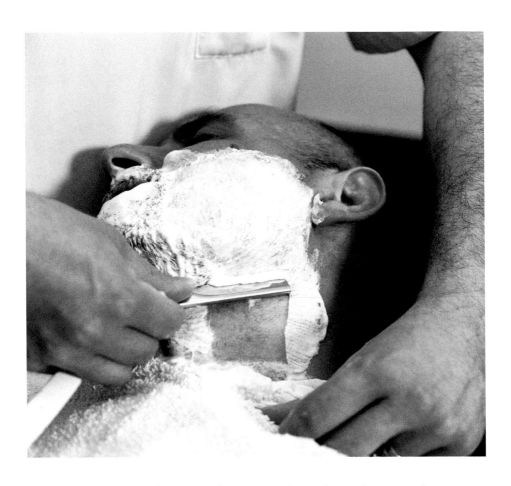

Men sometimes have the barber shave their **whiskers**.

Some women get **permanents** to make their hair curly.

This girl isn't sure she'll like her new haircut. She looks worried.

The barber makes her feel better.

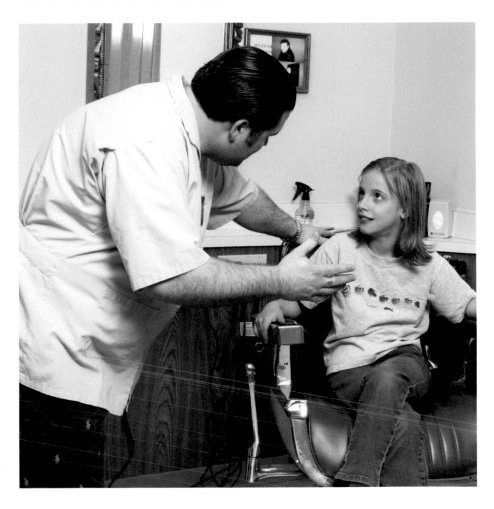

17

When you visit the barber, he puts a cape over your clothes. The cape keeps your clothes neat during the haircut.

The barber washes your hair. The barber uses **shampoo** to make your hair clean.

Next, you sit down in the barber's special chair.

The barber's chair has a **foot pedal**. It raises the chair so that the barber can reach your head easily.

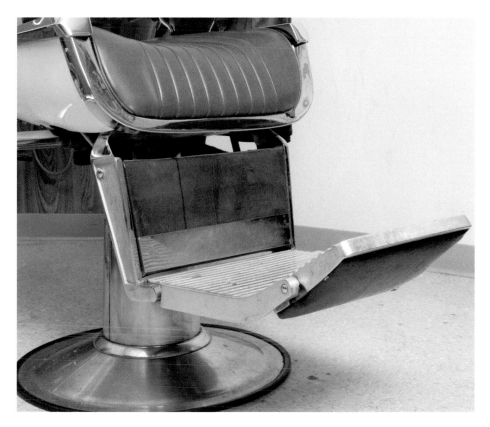

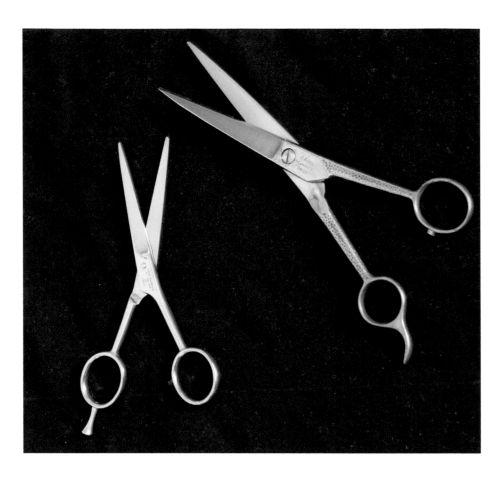

What tools does the barber use to cut
your hair?

He uses a
pair of
scissors.
Snip, snip!
He also might
use a razor.
Buzz! These
tools help
make your
hair look neat.

The barber makes sure the ends of
your hair are even.

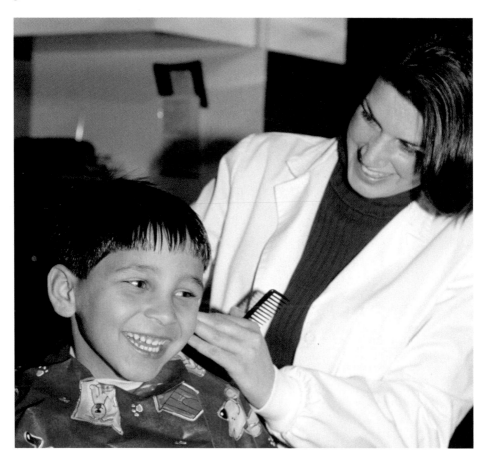

How does
it look?

The barber sweeps up your hair from around the chair. The shop is nice and clean for the next customer.

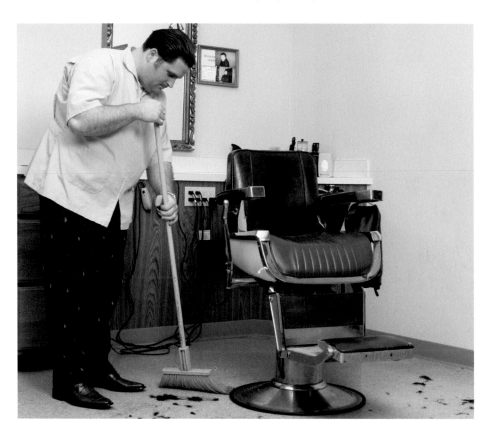

It's someone else's turn for a haircut.

Facts about Barbers

- Barbers are also called stylists and hairdressers. They may do many jobs for customers besides cutting hair. Some of these jobs include dying hair different colors and doing hair in fancy styles for special occasions. Cosmetologists also help people look their best. Their jobs include doing makeup and cutting and filing fingernails.

- Barbers have been around for thousands of years. The name "barber" comes from *barba*, the word for beard in the ancient language of Latin.

- Hair styles can change quickly. Being a barber means keeping track of what is in fashion and what customers will want.

- Have you ever heard of barbershop singing? A barbershop quartet is a group of four people who sing a style of music called barbershop.

Barbers through History

People have always needed haircuts. But the way that barbers do their job has changed over the years.

■ Long ago, barbers did more than cut hair and shave whiskers. They were also doctors and dentists. The striped barber's pole outside many modern shops dates back to those days. The red stripes represent blood, and the white stripes stand for bandages. Some people think that the blue stripes were added to match the U.S. flag.

■ In about 1700, the Russian emperor Peter the Great said that men with beards had to pay a tax. Russian barbers suddenly had lots of customers!

■ In the 1700s and 1800s, wigs were very popular, especially in Europe. Some barbers made wigs to stay in business.

More about Barbers

Check out these books and websites to learn more about barbers. Or visit a local barbershop and talk to a real barber!

Books

Davis, Kathryn Gibbs. *Katy's First Haircut*. Boston: Houghton Mifflin, 1985.

Landström, Olof, and Lena Landström. *Will Gets a Haircut*. Translated by Elisabeth Dyssegaard. New York: R & S Books, 1993.

Radabaugh, Melinda Beth. *Getting a Haircut*. Chicago: Heinemann, 2003.

Sirimarco, Elizabeth. *At the Barber*. Eden Prairie, MN: Child's World, 2000.

Tarpley, Natasha Anastasia. *Bippity Bop Barbershop*. Boston: Little, Brown, 2002.

Websites

BarberPole.com
   http://www.barberpole.com

National Cosmetology Association
   http://www.ncacares.org

Glossary

community: a group of people who live in the same city, town, or neighborhood. Communities share the same shops, schools, libraries, and other helpful places.

customers: people who buy something from a shop or store. Customers who visit barbers buy haircuts, shaves, permanents, and other services.

foot pedal: part of a barber's chair. The barber presses down on the pedal with his or her foot to raise or lower the chair.

permanents: treatments that make hair curly for a few months. Permanents are often called "perms" for short.

shampoo: soap for hair

training: classes that teach people how to do something

whiskers: the hair on a man's face

Index

Photo Acknowledgments

The photographs in this book appear courtesy of: © Royalty-Free/CORBIS, front cover; © Ted Horowitz/ CORBIS, p. 3; © Image Source/SuperStock, pp. 4, 5, 10, 11, 13, 14, 20, 27; © Christian Sarramon/CORBIS, p. 6; © Scott Barrow, Inc./SuperStock, p. 7; © Rob Lewine/CORBIS, p. 8; © Todd Strand/Independent Picture Service, pp. 9, 16, 17, 21, 22, 25, 26; © age fotostock/SuperStock, pp. 12, 18, 23; © Derrick A. Bruce/ CORBIS, p. 15; © Allen T. Jules/CORBIS, p. 19; © Jack Ballard/Visuals Unlimited, p. 24; © Roger Wood/ CORBIS, p. 29.